BREW IT
YOURSELF

by LEIGH P. BEADLE

BREW IT YOURSELF

MAKING FINE WINES AND
LIQUEURS AT HOME

Revised Edition

BREW IT YOURSELF

A COMPLETE GUIDE TO

THE BREWING OF

BEER, ALE, STOUT & MEAD

Leigh P. Beadle

FARRAR, STRAUS AND GIROUX
NEW YORK

To my wife, Becky, my favorite beer-drinking buddy

ACKNOWLEDGMENT

I would like to express my appreciation to those who have helped me in developing and refining the procedures used in this book to brew beers; to the research departments of breweries both here and abroad. Thanks are also due all those who have sampled these beers without knowing that they were not store-bought, so that I got a candid opinion on how best to develop the basic recipes.

CONTENTS

No nation is sober when the dearness of fermented malt drinks substitutes ardent spirits as the common beverage.

Thomas Jefferson

BREW IT
YOURSELF

Author's Note

The purpose of this book is to provide you with a complete, easy-to-follow guide to making superior beer in your own home. While there are several publications available from England and Europe on brewing, they tend to emphasize the heavier ales and stouts and rely on procedures that are unfamiliar to Americans. This book is unique in that most of the recipes are more attuned to the American preference for light lager beer. Contrary to popular belief, you can make a delicious, high-quality beer for a total outlay of two hours of your time and an initial cost of less than twenty-five dollars. This investment will provide you with permanent equipment and enough ingredients to make over five gallons of rich, refreshing beer. At today's prices for commercial beer, you will more than break even on your first two batches! Thereafter, your cost will come to less than five cents a bottle for American-style lager of premium quality and less than ten cents a bottle for beer that is clearly superior to the finest German imported variety. German and other imported beers sell for up to eighty cents a bottle in the better shops, so you can see that this is a hobby that will save you money. This book provides information on where to obtain all supplies and equipment for beermaking (the same equipment can be used to make wine.)*

The procedures for making beer are scientific, and factors that might cause variations in quality from batch to batch have been eliminated. Since fermentation is a natural process, you will be able to produce the highest-quality beer on your first attempt simply by following the instructions closely. The equipment for making beer is compact and convenient. All you will need is space enough for your fermentation vessel, which takes up no more room than a large wastebasket.

* See my companion book, *Making Fine Wines and Liqueurs at Home* (Farrar, Straus & Giroux, 1972).

Glossary of Brewing Terms

ALE

A fermented malt beverage in which top-fermenting yeast is used to carry out the fermentation.

ANAEROBIC FERMENTATION

Method of fermentation whereby air is prevented from coming into contact with the brew.

ASCORBIC ACID

Pure vitamin C. Used in beermaking at the rate of one half teaspoon to five gallons prior to bottling to prevent oxidation.

BARLEY

A grain from which malt is extracted for beermaking.

BOCK BEER
A specially brewed beer which is characteristically dark and heavy. It is made this way by caramelizing or toasting the malt.

BREW
A synonym for beer and ale and other beverages that undergo fermentation.

BREWERS' YEAST
A type of yeast, *Saccharomyces cerevisiae,* which has been cultured specifically for brewing beer. Not to be confused with the brewers' yeast sold in drugstores and supermarkets. That type is a dietary supplement composed of dead yeast cells and cannot be used for fermentation.

CARBON DIOXIDE
The gas produced by the action of yeast during fermentation.

CARBOY
A closed container used to insure an anaerobic fermentation. The secondary fermenter.

DEXTROSE
A basic sugar, also known as corn sugar. Sometimes used as a substitute for malt in brewing.

FERMENTATION
Process by which yeast acts on sugar to convert it to carbon dioxide gas and alcohol in approximately equal amounts.

FERMENTATION LOCK
A device to insure that carbon dioxide gas can escape from the carboy without allowing air to enter.

FININGS

Substance used to clear and settle beer and wine; forms a slight colloid solution in the brew. Generally gelatin.

GELATIN

See FININGS.

HEAD

The foamy top on all high-quality beers.

HEADING LIQUID

A liquid used by some brewers to put an artificial head on beer when insufficient malt is used to produce a genuine head. Highly undesirable among professional brewers of quality beer.

HOPS

An herb used to impart the characteristic bitter taste to beer and ale.

HYDROMETER

Device used by brewers to measure the amount of unfermented sugars remaining in the beer mix.

INVERT SUGAR

Similar to dextrose.

KILN

Large drum used to dry and warm barley malt.

LAGER

A clear, light-bodied beer. The word "lager" comes from the German word meaning "to store." Most American beers are the lager type.

MALT
Sugar formed from the starches inside the barley husk.

MALTOSE
Malt sugar which can be converted to alcohol and carbon dioxide gas by the action of the yeast.

NATURALLY CONDITIONED BEER
Beer whose carbonation is produced naturally by fermentation in a sealed bottle. It has a much greater character than the bulk-process or nondeposit beers. These latter beers are charged with carbon dioxide gas prior to bottling and make up the vast majority of the world's commercial beers. Home-brewed beer is naturally conditioned.

NUTRIENT
An essential additive in beermaking, usually diammonium phosphate, which insures that the yeast will carry on a vigorous ferment.

PILSNER
A term, synonymous with "lager," that denotes a light-bodied beer. The name was originally used by the brewery at Pilsen, Czechoslovakia.

PRIMARY FERMENTER
Vessel in which the primary, or tumultuous, fermentation takes place.

PRIMING
The addition of a small amount of dissolved household sugar to the beer just prior to bottling, to produce carbonation.

SACCHAROMYCES CEREVISIAE
Latin name for brewers' yeast.

SACCHAROMYCES ELLIPSOIDEUS
Latin name for wine yeast.

SECONDARY FERMENTER
Vessel in which the secondary fermentation takes place. Also called the carboy.

SIPHONING
Method by which liquid is transferred from one container to another. For siphoning to take place, the pouring end of the hose must be lower than the suction end.

SPRUCE ESSENCE
A natural spruce flavoring which was widely used in American beer during Colonial times and which is still used in some of the finest German and Scandinavian beers.

STOUT
A British dark beer that is very heavy. It generally has a high hop concentration.

SUGAR
In brewing, the malt sugar to be fermented.

WORT
The correct term for the beer mix prior to fermentation.

YEAST
The organism that converts sugar to alcohol and carbon dioxide gas during its reproductive cycle.

Background

Beermaking is one of the oldest arts known to man. Man, it is now believed, was brewing beer at the same time as he was learning the rudiments of making bread, for any number of grains which were used to make bread could easily have been transformed into beerlike drinks through the natural process of fermentation. Our earliest evidence indicates that barley malt was used in brewing by the Mesopotamians around 6000 B.C. The Egyptians were known to have practiced the art quite avidly around 2000 B.C. They are believed to have introduced spices and herbs—forerunners of the present-day hops—into their beer to counteract the sweet taste of the malts. From Egypt the Greeks carried the art to Europe, and the Romans learned about beer during their conquest of Greece. It is believed that beer was introduced to England by the Roman armies. Hops came into use in Europe as the main herb to complement the malt flavor, and the use of this bitter herb soon spread to England. Besides adding flavor to the beer, hops also acted as a preservative. The consumption of beer in England during the Middle Ages must have been enormous. Historical documents of the Duke of Lancaster indicate that he provided each of the ladies-in-waiting at his court with eight gallons of beer a week!

The importance of beer to the early colonizers of America is evidenced when the *Mayflower*, by an accident of navigation, landed at Plymouth Rock in Massachusetts instead of its intended destination of Virginia. In the *Pilgrim Journal* we read, "For we could not now take time for further search or consideration, our victuals being much spent, especially our beere."* Beer was stocked on long ocean voyages because it tended to retain its freshness, due to the preservative qualities of the hops, whereas water soon spoiled. Beer also provided the vitamins and minerals needed to fight diseases such as scurvy, which plagued ocean voyages. Early colonial governments recognized the healthful qualities of beer. The Virginia Assembly sent a proclamation to new colonists urging them to bring malt with them to "Brewe and drink beere, until their bodies were

---

* Reprinted from the *Encyclopedia Americana* (1967 edition) by permission of the publishers, Grolier Incorporated, New York.

hardened to the drinking of water." William Penn opened the first commercial brewery in Pennsylvania and George Washington maintained a brewery on his estate at Mount Vernon, where he was known as a master brewer of fine beers.

In the century following the Revolutionary War, a brewhouse was an essential part of the American household and brewing was encouraged by the government. In 1789 James Madison made a motion before the United States House of Representatives that the low duty of eight cents a barrel be placed on malt liquors, so that "this low rate will be such an encouragement as to induce the manufacture of beer in every state of the Union." A specific example of legislation to foster beer drinking in the early days of the republic is found in the Massachusetts Act of 1789, which states that "the wholesome qualities of malt liquors greatly recommend them to general use, as an important means of preserving the health of the citizens of this commonwealth, and of preventing the pernicious effect of spirituous liquors."

Around 1840 the types of beer brewed in this country began to change. Up until that time, the predominant brew was the traditional British-type ale, a strong, heavy, rather bitter drink with a high alcohol content, averaging around eight percent by weight, or higher. With the influx of German immigrants around the middle of the nineteenth century, however, a lighter, much milder beer began to be made here. The Germans set up breweries that made the lighter, milder, bottom-fermenting lagers typical of regions such as Bavaria. After the turn of the century, American tastes favored an even lighter beer.

One good reason for this tendency toward lightness is that the United States has a much warmer climate than Europe and we need a beer that will quench thirst, a beer that can be quaffed in fair quantities, without leaving us drunk in the process. Prohibition was also a factor in our turning to lighter beer. During this period, beer and wine, along with hard liquor, were prohibited, and breweries were forced to turn out a brew called "near beer," a very light beverage that contained less than one half of one percent alcohol by weight. Fortunately for those who prefer real beer, Prohibition ended with the enactment of the Twenty-first Amendment on December 5, 1933. After a long thirteen years ten months nineteen days seventeen hours and thirty-two and one half minutes, Americans could again step up to a bar for a real beer.

I had a discussion recently with an executive of one of the major brewing firms concerning the lightness of American beer. He told me something interesting about the trend to very light, dry beer following World War II. At that time, he said, women throughout the country began drinking beer. Many men were in military service, and with the pay scales at a rather meager level, they had only a limited amount of money to spend on dates when they could get a weekend pass. Most couples could just afford hot dogs and a pitcher of beer on their evenings of wining and dining. For the first time, women drank beer regularly, but they objected to the bitter taste. To make beer more enjoyable to women, then, it became the custom to dilute a pitcher of beer with a glass of ice water, to weaken the taste. After the war, beer became available at the local supermarket, where it was bought for home consumption, instead of at the local tavern. Since it was the women who did the buying, the breweries catered to their taste for the weaker, blander beer they had become accustomed to drinking during the war.

This is certainly a plausible explanation for the popularity in this country of ultra-light beers. We have found, however, that women do not object to the rich, strong taste of beer, only to its bitterness. All the women who have sampled the beer recipes in this book have preferred them to the bland commercial beer. They also appreciate the nonfattening quality of home-brewed beer.

American beers average about 3.5 percent alcohol by weight, although some regional beers and ales go as high as 5.5 percent. (An alcohol content of 3.5 percent by weight means that 3.5 percent of the total weight of the beer is pure alcohol.) They are mostly light in color, very dry, and contain a relatively high degree of carbonation. These characteristics give them their very good thirst-quenching qualities. To attain the dryness common to beer produced in this country, breweries have had to use other grains along with the barley malt in brewing, since barley used alone will give beer a richer, heavier taste. The two most common additional grains are corn and rice, which can also be used by themselves to produce beer. When Columbus first arrived in the New World, he noted that the Indians used corn to brew a drink similar to beer. In Japan today, rice is used to brew sake, a drink which we know as rice wine but which is more correctly identified as a noncarbonated rice beer.

In Northern Europe, barley malt is almost exclusively the basic grain in brewing. This gives European beer a richer, malty taste and adds a certain heaviness to it, but it makes it slightly less desirable as a thirst-quencher. The Germans in particular turn out a highly malted beer that has a characteristic sweetness. This sweetness is countered with a higher hop content, which adds bitterness to the brew. Among the most delicious beers available commercially are some of these German imports, known as "Sunday sipping beers"; also, beers imported from Denmark and Holland. These, incidentally, are the pilsner beers that were considered so light around the middle of the last century, so you can imagine the strength of the brews they were drinking in those days! The term "pilsner," which is used to describe the lighter beers, comes from Pilsen, a town in Czechoslovakia, where the Pilsen brewery has been in continuous operation for over eight hundred years. I've sampled some of their beer and it is delicious, with a rich but mellow taste. One reason for this taste is that the hops grown in Czechoslovakia and in Bavaria have a mellow flavor not generally found in hops grown in other regions of the world. Many American brewers, in fact, import these hops to use as a blend in brewing their beers. Some of the foreign breweries also use a greater amount of malt in their beers, which adds to the body. With some of the recipes in this book, you can virtually duplicate the flavor of the imported beers if your taste is for the heavier varieties of brew, and at a considerable saving in cost.

It should be noted that the strength of a beer's flavor is not necessarily due to its high alcohol content. At the risk of incurring the wrath of American tourists to Europe who protest to the contrary, continental brews average around five to six percent of alcohol by weight —half again as much as standard American beers, yet far less than the eight to fourteen percent claimed by our more avid quaffers of the continental brews. A word of advice: Your first inclination may be to increase the alcohol content of the beer recipes given in this book, because, "After all, this is the reason for brewing my own beer—to get a more potent brew." Don't stray too far from the recommended level of ingredients, however. There is a definite decrease in the taste and overall quality of beer when the alcohol content goes beyond six percent. The recipes in this book will produce between 4.7 and 6 percent alcohol, and this is a sufficient amount to complement the taste. The drinking patterns of the British are reflected in a beer whose alcohol content has been kept within reasonable limits. In England, unlike here, there is a wide choice of popular brews, from the mild and relatively weak pale ales to the strong stouts and porters. The alcohol content ranges from three percent for the lighter ales to nine percent for the heavier stouts. Yet the most popular drink among the British is light ale, for the simple reason that beer drinkers like the taste of beer and therefore like to drink large quantities without becoming intoxicated.

Home-Brewing in the United States

The home-brewing of beer gained a certain degree of popularity in America during Prohibition, when beer could not be purchased, and then during the Depression, when, out of economic necessity, people concocted their own brews. These early attempts at the brewer's art resulted more often than not in a beer that varied from awful all the way up to mediocre. Home-brewers simply did not have access to the proper ingredients and techniques. The standard procedure for making the home-brew of those days was to add one can of malt extract and four or five pounds of sugar to five or six gallons of water. (So far, so good; but after this we go downhill fast.) The final step was the addition of a packet of Fleischmann's yeast, to start the process of fermentation. This it does, but there is one problem. While Fleischmann makes an excellent yeast, it is bakers' yeast and there is a distinct difference between bakers' yeast and brewers' yeast. Bakers' yeast is cultured specifically for use in breadmaking. If used for brewing, it imparts a mustiness to the brew, making it taste yeasty. And because it does not settle out well, it leaves the beer looking cloudy. Do not make this mistake, or your efforts will result in a brew that is not at all satisfactory.

The type of yeast used by brewers is especially cultured for the purpose. It is developed for its ability to promote a vigorous fermentation, its tendency to impart a good lager taste to the beer, and its settling quality, which leaves the beer clear and sparkling. This yeast cannot be bought locally but is readily available through wine-makers' supply firms. The scientific name for it is *Saccharomyces cerevisiae*, "*cerevisiae*" being the Latin name for beer. In fact, there are regions in Europe, notably parts of France, where beer is called "cervoise" instead of the more common "bière."

If the early home-brewers in this country had only left out the sugar and used more malt, and if they had had access to brewers' yeast instead of bakers' yeast, the art of brewing your own beer might very well be far more widespread than it is, for, despite Grandpa's allegations to the contrary, his home-brew just didn't make the grade as a fine beer. The comment I get from people who sample my own beer who have tried the former variety is: "This is real beer, I thought you made home-brew!" The difference in terminology is a matter of semantics; the difference in taste is a matter of record.

There are several other factors which affect the quality of the beer you brew. These will be discussed in a later section. They include the quality of the water, the techniques used in mixing the ingredients, and the chemical additives that promote a healthy ferment. Before going into the technique of brewing your own beer, let us consider the methods used by commercial breweries, so we can correlate them with the procedures we shall use in our operation.

How Beer Is Produced Commercially

Four basic ingredients are required to produce lager beer. They are: malt extract, hops, water, and brewers' yeast. A brief description of how commercial breweries produce beer will point out the similarities and the differences between commercial procedures and the steps you will follow as a home-brewer.

The most complicated step for the commercial brewer is the preparation of the malt. This starts with fresh barely, which is a grain much like wheat. First it is cleaned, then saturated with water and placed in huge drums that revolve slowly at a rate of about one turn an hour. Thus the grain is aerated, and allowed to breathe, as it is now coming to life and germinating in the warm drums. Aeration also helps dispel the heat generated by the grain during the germination stage, which is considerable, since the drums may contain as much as 40,000 pounds of malt each. During the germination of the grain, malt is formed inside the husk. After six days, the maximum amount of malt has formed and further growth is ended by kiln-drying the barley seeds at a temperature of about 150° Fahrenheit. At this point, however, not all barley is of high enough quality for brewing beer. If the grains are not of sufficient size to produce a good-quality malt content, this barley is separated and used for distilling into whisky. Grains that are smaller still are used for livestock feed.

Once the barley grains have been kiln-dried, they are hard and brittle, ready for the cracking stage, during which they are cracked open by rollers. This allows the release of the malt when the cracked grains are boiled, during the mashing process. At this point the water and barley grains are kept at a temperature of 153° Fahrenheit for several hours, to set the enzymes and to convert the starches into sugar. The malt has now been completely separated from the spent grains, and hops are added to the malt water. This gives the beer, or "wort," as it is referred to at this stage, its characteristic bitter flavor. The hops also add aroma and impart certain preservative qualities. After the boiling process, when the necessary flavor has been extracted from the hops, and the wort has been sufficiently sterilized, the mixture is allowed to cool to below 70°. Thus the proper temperature is reached for the next stage, which is the addition or "pitching" of the yeast, *Saccharomyces cerevisiae.*

Breweries maintain carefully nurtured yeast colonies in their laboratories, as the quality of beer depends to a large extent on the quality of the yeast. In some breweries, in fact, the cultures are extracted from the bottom of the storage tanks and used in succeeding batches. The yeast, which is in a thick layer, is made up of three sections. The top is composed mainly of dead yeast cells; the bottom, of immature cells; and the middle layer, of the lively, active yeast cells. It is from the middle layer that future yeast cultures are taken.

After the yeast has been pitched, the wort begins the stage of tumultuous fermentation. At this point the yeast is most vigorous and rapidly converts the malt sugars into alcohol and carbon dioxide. It is during the period of rapid fermentation that the sugary wort is transformed into beer. After about a week, the frothing, bubbling fermentation begins to slow down, and the beer is transferred into large storage, or lagering, tanks. The fermentation is then only half complete. It continues at a much slower rate in the tanks for another five to eight weeks. One reason why the rate of fermentation is slower is that most of the sugars have already been converted during the primary fermentation; also, the storage tanks are kept at a temperature of about 33° Fahrenheit, and the cooler the temperature, the slower the yeasts work. It is this cold storage that gives the beer its mellow lager taste. During the lagering of beer, clarifiers (beer finings) are sometimes added to help carry sediment and yeast particles to the bottom and give the beer its clear, sparkling look. Small amounts of gelatin are usually used as finings. They form a colloid solution in the beer which gradually settles to the bottom, carrying all particles with it. The final step in the commercial brewing process is to siphon the beer from the tanks and then to charge it with carbon dioxide gas just before bottling. This gives beer its carbonation, which enhances the taste and produces the characteristic foamy head when it is poured.

Bottled beer may be either regular or "draft." Regular beer is pasteurized at a temperature of 140° F. for twenty minutes before bottling. This is done by passing the beer through heated pipes on the way to the bottles. Beer that is to be draft in bottles is passed through a millipore filter, to prevent yeast from entering the bottle. Both processes prevent continued fermentation in the bottles. The beer has already been charged with the correct amount of carbonation before bottling. If fermentation were to continue inside the sealed bottle, more carbon dioxide would form and the bottle would burst. Draft beer that is to be put into barrels does not have to be filtered, as it is kept under refrigeration to prevent any significant fermentation. Besides, the barrels would withstand a much higher pressure than bottles.

"Draft," with reference to beer, has a different meaning in England and in parts of Europe than it does here.

As indicated, we use the term to denote a nonpasteurized beer. On the other side of the ocean, however, draft means noncarbonated. All American beer is well carbonated, but this is not always the case overseas. Some European home-brewing books concentrate on the noncarbonated variety and mention carbonation only as an afterthought. I've tried some of the European "draft" beers, and some of the home recipes for them, and, rest assured, they are as bad as you imagine them to be. They are not included in this book.

Now that we have followed the commercial brewing process, we are ready to consider the method you will use to achieve the same end. You will find our methods just as scientific, though much simpler, and the results quite extraordinary.

Equipment

All the equipment and ingredients needed to brew beer can be obtained in one kit through the winemakers' supply firm listed in the back of this book, and the total outlay for equipment and ingredients should be less than twenty-five dollars. Considering the cost of store-bought beverages, you will more than break even on your first two batches of beer. Thereafter the cost per five-gallon batch of beer will be less than five or ten cents a bottle, depending on the particular recipe you use.

You will need the following equipment:

TWO-GALLON MIXING POT

You may already have one of these in your kitchen, but I would recommend buying a new one to use exclusively for brewing. The one you already own will have trace elements of soap and grease film from previous use, and these two substances, no matter how slight the amounts, should never come into contact with your brewing utensils, as they adversely affect the flavor of beer. The light aluminum pot with wire handles available at any supermarket is quite satisfactory. It costs less than two dollars.

PRIMARY FERMENTER

This is the container in which the primary, or tumultuous, fermentation takes place. There are several different types of containers available. These include earthenware crocks made for the purpose, and large glass bottles—both of which should be avoided. They are heavy, which makes them difficult to work with, and quite breakable, sometimes with painful consequences, as I found out the hard way! They are also difficult to keep clean, and cleanliness, as we shall see in a later section, is paramount in good brewing. A very suitable container of the type I use is offered in the kit supplied by the wine-making supply firm listed on page

109. It is made of an inert plastic which will impart no taste to the brew, and is naturally the correct size.

SECONDARY FERMENTER

This is a plastic "carboy" fitted with a fermentation lock. It is also included in the kit and is of the dimensions required for the recipes listed in this book.

FERMENTATION LOCK

This is purchased with the carboy. It is a device to insure that no air can reach the brew during the secondary fermentation, while at the same time allowing the carbon dioxide to escape. Since beer will spoil just as surely as milk from contact with air, we must insure a totally anaerobic ferment throughout. The lock is filled with water to a depth of only one half inch prior to inserting the cap. When the lock is fitted to the carboy, a very slight pressure is created inside by the formation of carbon dioxide. The gas escapes by bubbling through the water in the lock. Lifting the carboy during the secondary fermentation should be avoided if possible, as this will create a reverse pressure that will suck air and water into the vessel through the lock.

You may ask at this point: "Why use a primary fermenter at all, why not just ferment in the secondary fermenter?" Well, if the foam generated during the first day of fermentation were produced in the confined area of the carboy, it would clog the fermentation lock, seep through it, and make a nice foamy arrangement on the floor, leaving you in danger of having your equipment and yourself removed by your irritated wife.

SIPHONING HOSE

This piece of equipment is needed to transfer the beer from container to container and into the bottles. The brew cannot be poured, as that would upset the yeast sediment and prevent the clarifying of the beer. Figure 5 shows how to cut off the flow to avoid spillage during the bottling process. You may come across siphon sets that have complicated features such as shut-off clamps and automatic siphon pumps. These are expensive, and they are difficult to clean. Also, they do not work as well as the method illustrated. The correct kind of hose with rigid attachment is included in the fermentation kit I've recommended here.

MISCELLANEOUS ITEMS

You will also need the following, which you very likely have around the house already: large roll of Scotch or masking tape; extra-wide box of Saran Wrap (or you can use the plastic sheeting placed on clothing by dry cleaners); measuring cup; small saucepan; long plastic spoon; and candy thermometer (optional).

BOTTLES

Using the standard fermentation kit for brewing, you will need 55 twelve-ounce bottles. If you use quart bottles you will need 22. Using fifth-size bottles requires 26. Be sure to use only brown- or green-tinted bottles. The tint filters out light rays; this is crucial in beer-making. If beer is exposed to light for an appreciable length of time, the flavor will be affected, due to photo-synthesis. There are two methods available for sealing your bottles. You could bottle in quart or fifth sizes only, using the screw-top beer- or soft-drink bottles. These can be made gas-tight if you use a rubber gripping cloth to insure that the cap is sealed tightly. Do not use bottles with the smaller screw caps that are only regular bottle caps crimped over a slightly threaded neck. These are not gas-tight when resealed. While using quart- and fifth-size bottles saves the cost of a capper, there is one disadvantage. You must pour home-brewed beer from the bottle all at once in one smooth, uninter-rupted flow; otherwise, the slight yeast layer on the bottom of the bottle will be disturbed and cloud the beer somewhat. If you use the larger bottles, you may not want to pour that much beer at one time; there-fore, it is best to use the tall, returnable twelve-ounce bottles and buy a capper and caps. The returnable bottles are becoming available again as people are beginning to appreciate the tremendous waste and litter problem created by thoughtless individuals who dispose of the throw-away bottles and cans all over the national landscape. If your supermarket does not have them yet, you can easily talk the local tavern-owner into selling you three cartons of empty bottles for about one dollar a carton. Keep the cartons for storage purposes. It is important from a safety standpoint that you do not use disposable twelve-ounce bottles, as they are much weaker than the returnable ones and some could burst. The disposable quart- and fifth-size bottles are no problem, however. Cappers and caps are available through wine-making supply firms such as the one listed in back of the book and cost under ten dollars for the best around.

THE HYDROMETER

Although the procedures suggested in this book will produce in almost all instances the correct amount of carbonation in your beer, there is always the possibility of some variation in the amount of time needed for the beer to completely ferment out. Cold temperatures or a higher or lower than normal mineral content in the water could cause the beer to ferment slower than indicated. If this is the case and you add the priming sugar to beer that still has an excess of malt sugar to ferment, you risk a burst bottle, since fermentation continues after the cap is sealed. With a hydrometer, however, you eliminate the possibility of over- or under-carbonation.

The hydrometer you use should be one designed specifically for fermentation, such as the one included in the fermentation kit suggested. This device simply measures the amount of sugar remaining in the brew to be fermented. Figure 6 will show you how to use it. You can either remove the fermentation lock and insert the hydrometer into the beer after the fifteen-day fermentation, or you can remove some beer by carefully lowering a small juice glass into the beer and fill your testing jar. Either way, there is no danger of spoiling your beer as long as you rinse the hydrometer or glass with water just before use. The air cannot get to the beer, because of the protective layer of carbon dioxide gas resting on the top of the brew. This does not rush out when the lock is removed, since it is heavier than air, and in almost every case the beer will be ready to bottle at this point, anyway. If the beer does need to work out a few more days and you refit the lock, the small amount of air trapped inside will soon be expelled through the lock.

Let's look again at Figure 6. The hydrometer on the left shows a reading of 1.042. This is a standard reading for the beer mix just before the start of fermentation. Water would show a reading of 1.000. Since the beer mix contains sugar, which is heavier than water, the stem will float higher, giving a reading greater than 1.000. The hydrometer on the right shows a typical reading for beer that has aged two weeks in the carboy, just before the priming sugar is added. The reading is 1.010—the final specific gravity of some of the recipes. Each recipe in this book has listed with it a specific gravity which should be attained after fermentation in the carboy. If the reading is greater than this listed specific gravity—for instance, 1.014 instead of 1.010— you would know that the beer should remain in the carboy to ferment for several more days, until it approaches 1.010. It will then be ready to prime with two-fifths of a cup of sugar and bottle. Occasionally you may have a batch that will not quite work down to the final figure even after an additional few days in the carboy. This is sometimes the case when powdered malt is used and is due to the variable amounts of insoluble sugars in the malt, or it may be that you let the temperature of the water rise above 140° F. when mixing the ingredients. If this happens and the fermentation lock is not bubbling at a rate that shows active fermentation, it is safe to prime and bottle. When using the hydrometer, be sure to insert the stem into the jar with a spinning motion, to prevent any bubbles from adhering to the side of the float, as this would give an incorrect reading. The final specific gravity readings in the recipes are already corrected for an assumed room temperature of 70°. The problem of slow fermentation may never arise in your brewing, of course, since the procedures outlined here are very thorough. But this is the extra touch of professionalism in your brewing that will eliminate problems, should they arise. After all, you will want to impress your friends with your newly acquired skill, and they may look askance at your brewing abilities if you walk into the room carrying a sealed bottle of your best brew as if it were a live grenade!

Ingredients

MALT EXTRACT

The main recipes in this book call for the use of two types of malt extract, either hop-flavored malt syrup in cans or dried malt extract, which is in powdered form. Some of the recipes call for a combination of both. After trying all the many brands of foreign and domestic malts available, I have found that the very finest beer is made using the Munton & Fison, Ltd., brand. This popular British malt is available through wine- and beer-makers' supply firms. The firm listed in back of the book will provide you with the address of the closest outlet, or you can order it direct from them by mail. The canned malt syrup is hop-flavored, which eliminates a step in the brewing operation. You don't have to prepare hops or hop extract separately in the brew. It is

packed in one-kilo quantities (2.2 lbs.) and two cans
are required per five-gallon batch. The hop flavoring in
two cans is exactly right for a batch this size. The dried
malt extract made by Munton & Fison, like their canned
syrup, is also extremely high in quality. It achieves a
degree of total fermentability, due to its high maltose
content. The dried malt is not hop-flavored, so you must
add hops or hop extract to those recipes which call for
dried malt extract without the canned malt syrup. Beers
made with the dried malt have a very pleasing character, and since you are adding your own hops, you can
achieve an endless variation in the type of beer you
make. Both the canned syrup and dried malt extract are
available in light or dark, depending on your tastes.
Buying the malt in syrup or dried form is most convenient for the home beer maker, since the complicated
steps of cracking and mashing the barley grains, described in the chapter on commercial procedures, have
already been accomplished. You simply pour the malt
into your container of warm water and dissolve it. A
word of advice on dried malt extract. Do not use dried
light malt made in the U.S. The only light malt currently
made in this country is a bakery malt and contains only
20% malt extract and 80% dried corn extract, partially
non-fermentable. The Munton & Fison dried malt is
100% malt extract and the corn sugar (dextrose) which
the recipes call for in addition to the malt extract is
completely fermentable. If the domestic bakery malt
is used, the beer will lack body and the final specific

gravity will be too high, due to the non-fermentable corn extracts.

There is one very important point I should make concerning the mixing of the malt, which I will again emphasize in the section on procedures. Do not bring the water to a boil. You will remember from the section on commercial procedures that the malt was kept at a temperature of 153° F. to allow the diastase enzyme to convert starches to sugar for correct fermentation of the malt, then boiled to stabilize the mix. This procedure has also been accomplished with the canned malt syrup and the dried malt and does not need to be repeated. You should not heat the water to more than 150°. This is sufficient to completely dissolve the malt. If you were to bring the water to a boil, then add it to the remaining four gallons of cold water in the batch, it would still heat up the entire batch, so that you would have to wait many hours before adding the yeast. Since it is important to get the fermentation going as fast as possible to prevent the malt from souring, it is better to heat the water to only 150° F. This way, there is no delay and you can add the yeast as soon as the mix is added to the remaining cold water in the batch.

CORN SUGAR

Corn sugar, also known as dextrose, is a necessary ingredient in all high-quality lager beers. Generally speaking, malt extract provides the body, hops the bitterness, and corn sugar the strength. You will note that in all the beer recipes in this book the total amount of malt extract and corn sugar always adds up to six pounds for each five-gallon batch. If six pounds of malt extract were used, the alcoholic content would still be acceptable but the body and flavor would be far too heavy for normal tastes. If the malt were reduced to around three and one half pounds without adding any corn sugar, the taste and body would be fairly acceptable but the alcoholic content would be too low. Corn sugar is almost totally fermentable and does not have the heaviness which characterizes malt extract; therefore, it is a necessary adjunct when making a lager-style beer. All commercial breweries use either rice or corn as their adjunct. A highly desirable feature of the Munton & Fison canned malt syrup is that it is blended with a small amount of glucose, also a corn sugar, to adjust the flavor to lager-beer requirements. Even so, it is necessary to add a certain amount of corn sugar so that the correct ratio is achieved for our five-gallon batches. Never use household sugar in place of corn sugar, as this will give the beer a sharp, cidery taste.

HOPS

This ingredient will not have to be purchased for our main recipes. For those who become experienced in home-brewing and would like to try some variations, I have included some recipes calling for the addition of hops separately. Hops are a pungent herb that flavors beer with a bitter taste to counteract the sweetness of the malt. Hops also act as a preservative and add aroma to the beer. Only the leaves of the female hop plant, *Humulus lupulus*, are used in brewing. The male plant imparts an unpalatable flavor and is even outlawed (except for a few sufficient to fertilize female flowers) in many countries which produce significant quantities of hops for brewing. Hops can be purchased in four-ounce compressed packets through wine-makers' supply firms. You can also buy hop extract from these same suppliers and add it directly to the brew without having to go to the trouble of preparing it by boiling.

A NOTE ON THE USE OF SPRUCE ESSENCE

Spruce essence, as the name implies, is simply a concentration of the essential oils of spruce twigs and leaves in liquid form. Spruce was used as a flavoring agent in beer during Colonial times much the same as hops are used today, to counteract the sweetness of the malt and to round out the flavor of good beer. The finest German beers even today are flavored with spruce, along with the hops, to give them their world-renowned taste. American breweries have not used spruce in their beers since the last century. I have found that the use of spruce essence in very small amounts, only one teaspoon per five-gallon batch, rounds out the flavor of home-made beer perfectly and gives it a taste equal or superior to any beer you can buy regardless of the price. You will note that in many of the recipes I have included the use of spruce essence as an optional ingredient. I recommend it highly, especially for those of you who like the flavor of rich German beer.

FERMENTATION YEAST

The quality of the yeast is a major factor in determining the quality of the beer. The yeast available in grocery stores is not suitable for fermentation, only for baking. You should use a fast-starting dried fermentation yeast for beer-making, available through winemakers' supply firms. It has been cultured specifically for fermentation under scientifically pure laboratory conditions, and it comes in granule form, which is easy to use. There are some so-called pure beer yeast cultures available, also in granule form, which take two days or more to become active after adding them to the beer mix, unless you use a starter solution to get them going. These should not be used; you must specify a fast-starting beer yeast. The reason is that the malt in the beer mix will sour in the same manner as milk will sour if left too long. In the case of malt, twenty-four hours is sufficient time for it to start souring unless a protective layer of carbon dioxide gas has formed over it. This protective layer will form when active fermentation begins. A good fermentation yeast will begin active fermentation within about ten hours after adding it to the mix, and there will be absolutely no chance of spoilage of your batch when this happens. Some may argue that the slower-starting beer yeasts can be used if they are first activated in a starter solution before adding them to the beer mix. This will not entirely prevent the chance of spoilage, because the starter solution is also made up of malt and it can spoil quite easily during the two-to-four-day dormancy period of the yeast. If you use a good fast-acting dried beer yeast, such as the British Grey-Owl, you will never have a spoiled batch and the fermentation will be carried out very rapidly.

You may come across advertisements for various liquid yeasts. These should be avoided. I have ordered several of these and either the yeast has been contaminated and soured or the vials have been broken or damaged during shipment and the contents evaporated. Best to stay with the dried fermentation yeast to insure a consistently excellent ferment. You may hit upon the idea of reclaiming some of the yeast from each batch and storing it for use in succeeding batches. While some people do this, I would not recommend it. With the problems of exposure to air and of establishing a totally sterile environment for storing the extra yeast, the yeast sometimes spoils and the quality is always diminished. If you want to economize a little, the best way is to use only one half of a packet of yeast each time and carefully wrap up the rest. This has no effect on the ferment and you can get two batches from one box of yeast.

ADDITIVES

There are several additives which we mix into the beer at various stages to aid in fermentation or in preserving the quality of the beer.

SALT

This is used to aid in yeast fermentation and also to add to the body of the beer. Most beer recipes call for only two teaspoonfuls of salt per five gallons so there will be no perceptible flavor of salt in the end product.

ACID BLEND

Acid blend aids in fermentation by helping yeast break down the sugars into alcohol and carbon dioxide. Its acidity acts as a vitamin replenishment for the yeast. Acid blend can be purchased in powdered form at a nominal cost from wine-makers' supply firms. One teaspoonful of acid blend is added to every five gallons of beer, making it only a trace element so that no acid taste is imparted to the brew. Some home-brewers use the juice of half a lemon as a substitute for the acid, and this is acceptable; but your results will be much more satisfactory if you use the powdered form.

NUTRIENT

Nutrient is added to the beer mix in the fermenter at the same time as the yeast is added. Yeast requires sustenance to carry out its reproductive activity, as I'm sure we all do, and the nutrient acts to invigorate the yeast to carry out a uniform fermentation. It is usually composed of diammonium phosphate. This additive is also available through the wine-makers' suppliers.

FINING POWDER

This substance is added to the beer in very small quantities—only one half teaspoonful per batch is required. It is used to clarify the beer by carrying yeast particles to the bottom.

ASCORBIC ACID

To prevent oxidation due to contact with the air, ascorbic acid is added before bottling. One of the secrets of good brewing is to keep the beer from contact with air during fermentation. Since exposure to air cannot be avoided during the siphoning of the beer into bottles, we have to add one half teaspoonful of ascorbic acid. Along with our other measures, this will insure that we turn out quality batches each time with no variations.

SUGAR

One of the reasons for the rich flavor obtained from the beer recipes in this book is that household sugar is never used as a main ingredient. As mentioned earlier, the use of household sugar gives a sharp, cidery taste. The malt and corn sugars alone supply the required flavor and alcohol content. We do need a small amount of household sugar, however, to "prime" or carbonate the beer. This is done just before bottling. Two-fifths measuring cup of white household sugar dissolved in some of the beer which has been heated (not boiled) in a saucepan will allow the yeast to work further in the bottle to produce one-fourth percent more alcohol and sufficient carbon dioxide to carbonate the beer to the same extent as the commercial variety. (See Figure 7.)

WATER

The quality of the water is of prime importance in brewing a high-quality beer. Many of the world's best breweries are located in areas where high-quality water is available. Some breweries even pipe their water in from hundreds of miles away just to be sure of getting the highest-quality water. You may not be so fortunate as to have access to such high-quality water in your area, but this is seldom a problem. If the available water has a reasonably good taste, go ahead and use it. It will make a fine beer. If it has a decidedly mineral taste, as does some water near the coasts, you may need to find an alternate source. You may have firms in your area that specialize in providing good drinking water to homes and office water coolers. You can arrange with them to fill up your carboy at a nominal cost. Another effective alternative is to purchase a small water filter from one of the health-food stores. These filters remove most of the minerals from the water, and the cost is less than five dollars. Don't worry if your water has a chlorine taste. It will dissipate during the first day of active fermentation and will not affect the beer in any way.

CLEANING

It is very important to keep all your beermaking equipment absolutely clean. This must be done with hot water only. No soap or other detergent must ever come into contact with your containers, brushes, or bottles, because their chemical composition will lower the quality of your beer. It is virtually impossible to rinse off all soaps from your materials. A microscopic film always remains, and this is all that is needed to affect the taste of beer and wine. The same applies to your drinking mugs. Rinse them out with hot water only and stand them upside down to dry. Never use a cloth or anything else to dry them, as it will leave small particles which will affect the head of the beer.

This also applies to your other equipment. It is a

good idea to fill your new secondary fermenter halfway with very hot water and a one-pound box of baking soda. Let it sit for several hours, turn it over for another few hours, then pour the solution into the primary fermenter and let it sit awhile. This cleans out the industrial film common to polyethylene. The fermenters should then be thoroughly rinsed out with hot water. Thereafter, a hot-water rinsing immediately after each use (with the hand sprayer on the kitchen sink if you have one) will clean them out sufficiently. The baking-soda rinse should be repeated after every fifth batch to keep the containers fresh. Always store the secondary fermenter on its side, without a cap on the opening. Buy a small hand brush to clean out the hop ring from the primary fermenter after each use. As with the containers, beer bottles should be cleaned out immediately after emptying. Yeast and beer are very hard to remove if given a chance to dry out. Use the hand spray with hot water to rinse out the yeast layer on the bottom of the bottle completely, and then use the bottle brush, while the bottle is full of hot water, to clean out the inside completely. Empty and rinse out once more with the spray and leave upside down to dry. Be sure to store your bottles upside down to prevent any dust from settling in them between fillings. Rinse out your siphon hose immediately after use, or it will become messy on the inside, and if this happens, it cannot be cleaned out.

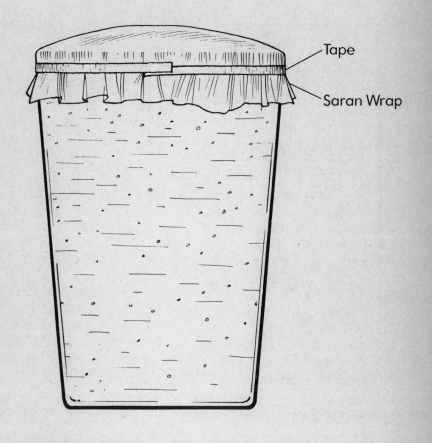

FIGURE 1

Primary fermenter

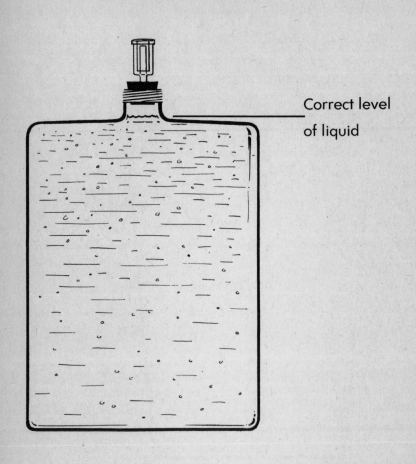

Correct level
of liquid

FIGURE 2

Secondary fermenter (carboy) with fermentation lock attached

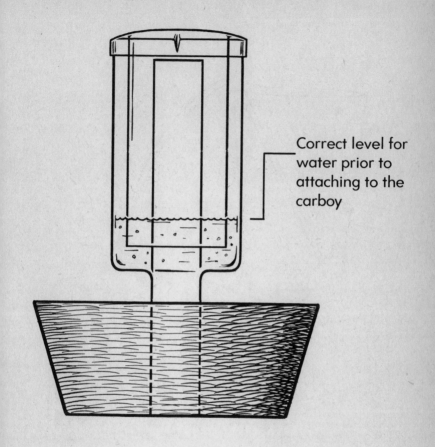

Correct level for water prior to attaching to the carboy

FIGURE 3

Fermentation lock

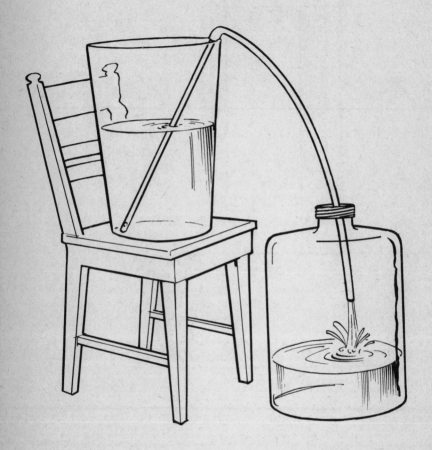

FIGURE 4

Siphoning. To start the flow of beer, suck on the lower end as you would on a straw until the flow is established. The flow end must be kept lower than the drawing end for the flow to continue

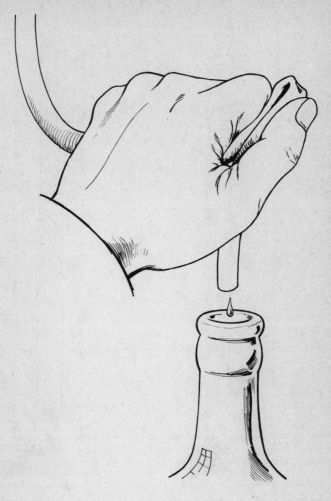

FIGURE 5

Example of how to cut off the flow of siphoning tube to avoid spillage when bottling

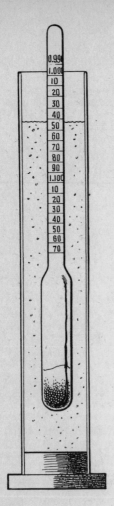
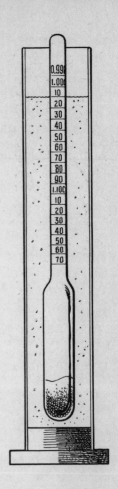

FIGURE 6

Left: *Example of hydrometer reading of 1.042. This is the average specific gravity of beer before yeast is added*

Right: *Hydrometer reading of 1.010—typical level after beer has been two weeks in the carboy. Sugar has almost completely worked out, so that beer is now lighter*

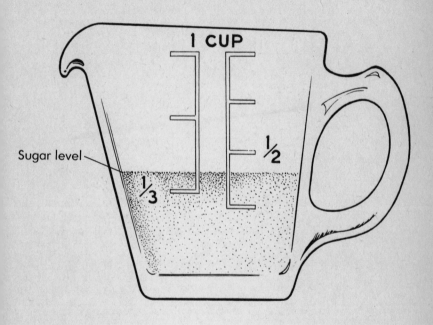

Sugar level

FIGURE 7

Since measuring cups do not have a 2/5 level, use a point mid-
way between 1/2 cup and 1/3 cup

Procedure for Beer

Now that you have an understanding of the mechanics of brewing and of the use of the equipment and ingredients, you can proceed to bring all these together to produce a sparkling, rich mug of beer which will impress your family and friends and, most important, yourself.

The first step is to fill the five-gallon secondary fermenter with water to a point one inch below the top. Use the seam of the fermenter as the water line for the correct amount, as it just happens to be an inch from the top. This gives you exactly 5¼ gallons of water, which is the amount called for in all the recipes in this book.* Transfer about one gallon of water from the

---

* All five-gallon containers—including five-gallon bottles—have a capacity of 5½ gallons. To fill the secondary fermenter completely

secondary fermenter to the two-gallon mixing pot, heat it to 150° F., and then remove the water from heat. (If you do not have a candy thermometer, estimate the temperature.) This is all the heat that is required for your mixing. Mix in one level teaspoonful of acid blend and the amount of salt called for in the particular recipe you are using, and stir. As you will remember, this chemically prepares the water for the correct fermentation of the malt.

Next, add the malt to the pot and stir it until it completely dissolves. If you are making a recipe calling for the use of dried malt along with canned malt, be sure to add the dried malt first and dissolve it completely. If the canned is added first, the dried malt will form lumps when added to the mix and it will take forever to dissolve. You will notice that when canned malt is poured into the pot it sinks to the bottom. This is one reason for removing the pot from the heat before adding the malt. Otherwise, some of the malt would be burned on the bottom of the pan and would impart an unpleasant taste to the beer. Add the corn sugar; dissolve.

After you have dissolved the malt and corn sugar and stirred the mix for about three minutes, pour the rest of the water from the carboy into the primary fermenter. Then pour the contents of the mixing pot into the primary fermenter and stir in. The total mix should now be

---

with the beer mix, use 5¼ gallons of water; the ingredients will take up the other quarter of a gallon.

cool enough to add the yeast, since only about one fifth of the water was heated. Cut open yeast packet and pour contents into a cup of *cold* water. After ten minutes stir yeast lumps entirely into solution and stir yeast solution thoroughly into beer mix in the primary fermenter. Make sure that the yeast doesn't come into contact with the heated water by itself. Yeast is a living thing and living things do not like to be boiled to death.

Add two level teaspoonfuls of nutrient. When the yeast and the nutrient have been added, or "pitched" as the process is known by commercial breweries, cover the fermenter, as shown in Figure 1, with a sheet of extra-wide Saran Wrap or similar plastic, and attach a single ribbon of masking or Scotch tape around the top to fasten it tightly.

Cover the fermenter with a towel to keep out the light. You will notice that within ten hours after adding the yeast the plastic sheeting will begin to billow. This is perfectly normal and is the result of the positive pressure of carbon dioxide gas filling the fermenter from the action of the yeast. This creates an anaerobic environment (one without air), which is necessary in brewing because the bacteria that spoil beer and other foods are mainly airborne and cannot live in a carbon dioxide environment. If you look into the fermenter, you may see a layer of light-colored foam on the surface. This is composed mainly of resins and essential oils from the hops (usually part of the malt mixture), which are forced to the surface by the carbon dioxide bubbles. Some books incorrectly advocate skimming off this foam, but this should never be done, because these oils and resins are what will later give the beer its body, aroma, and characteristic beer taste. This foamy layer may dissipate by the morning after you add the yeast, so don't be concerned if you never see it. The foam may leave a faint film around the primary fermenter just above the liquid as an indication that the tumultuous fermentation has taken place.

One day after the head recedes is the ideal time to transfer the mix to the secondary fermenter, or carboy. First sprinkle one half teaspoonful of finings into one half cup of hot water in a small saucepan and let it sit for ten minutes until it dissolves; then heat to just below boiling to mix the finings completely, stirring continuously. Rinse out the carboy with very hot water to clean it thoroughly. Have the finings solution close at hand before beginning your siphoning. Siphon the beer from the primary fermenter into the carboy. About halfway through the siphoning, add the finings mix; this will insure an even distribution. It is not necessary to interrupt the flow when you add the finings. Try not to spill any of the finings mix on your siphon hose or on the neck of the carboy; it's rather sticky. Be sure that during the siphoning you don't suck up too much of the sediment from the bottom of the fermenter. You will be able to siphon out all but the last half inch or so; this will fill your carboy to the correct height, which is just below the neck.

Lift the carboy onto a stool and then fit the fermentation lock, as shown in Figure 2. This lock must be filled with water to a depth of only one half inch prior to inserting the cap. After attaching it to the carboy, cover the carboy with a towel to keep out the light. Attach a slip of paper to the carboy noting the date, and let the brew work out for fifteen days at normal room temperature—around 70° F.

During this secondary fermentation, the brew will work out to the point where there is little or no sugar left for the yeast to convert to alcohol and carbon dioxide gas. Do not be concerned if you do not notice any bubbling of the fermentation lock. With the fast-acting beer yeasts now available, almost the entire fermentation will be completed during the primary fermentation. In fact, the specific gravity of the beer may have reached 1.010 or close to that reading when you transferred the beer to the carboy. Nevertheless, you must allow it to age the full fifteen days in the carboy so that the beer can mellow and begin to clear. After fifteen days in the carboy check with the hydrometer to be sure that the beer has worked out to approximately the specific-gravity reading indicated for that recipe. It may read even lower than specified, but this is no problem. If it is appreciably higher, let the fermentation continue for several more days, but this very seldom happens.

Rinse out the primary fermenter with hot water and drop in one half teaspoonful of ascorbic acid. This will prevent the beer from being affected by contact with the air. Siphon the beer into the primary fermenter, being careful not to disturb the yeast layer on the bottom of the carboy. While siphoning, pour some of the beer into a small saucepan and heat without boiling. Add exactly two fifths level measuring cup of white household sugar (Figure 7) and stir until thoroughly dissolved. Add this sugar solution to the beer in the primary fermenter and mix with a long plastic spoon to insure an even distribution. This is called priming the beer, and it will give us the same degree of carbonation as that in commercial beer. As you may already realize, it is imperative that the beer be allowed to work out for the full fifteen days, or longer if called for, or the sugar content after adding the priming sugar may be higher than necessary. The ideal room temperature for fermentation is between 60° and 70°. If this range is maintained, the fermentation should proceed as indicated. Try not to let the room temperature rise much above 70°. The chance of spoilage, while remote, is increased with a rise in temperature. As for the possibility of having to let the brew work out for more than the fifteen-day period, the only instance I can think of for a slower-than-normal fermentation is if your brewing temperature falls below 60° during the fermentation. In any case, the hydrometer removes all the guesswork.

Have your bottles completely cleaned, rinsed, and ready for use. If they are newly acquired, make sure they have been completely scrubbed out with your bottle brush and very hot water. If you have a dishwasher, it is a good idea to sterilize your bottles in it without detergent. Thereafter, sterilization is not necessary if you rinse them out immediately after emptying and scrub them with the bottle brush.

Siphon the beer from the primary fermenter into the bottles. Note Figure 5 for the method of cutting off the flow. Simply bend the tubing with your thumb. Fill the bottles to the standard height of all bottled beer—about an inch and a half from the top. Cap the bottles and tip them upside down once to wet the seals. The beer will look dark and cloudy at this point, but it will become clear and light over the next two weeks. Place them upright in their cartons and store at room temperature for at least fifteen days. On the fifth day after bottling, just to add the professional touch, give each bottle a sharp turn of the wrist clockwise and counterclockwise to shake loose the small particles of yeast adhering to the side and allow them to settle. When you do this, don't shake the bottle vertically or you will disturb the bottom layer of yeast too much.

Fifteen days after capping, the beer will be carbonated. Before this time it will have a sweet, flat taste and will do no justice to your efforts as a brewer. After the minimum aging period of fifteen days, your beer will be tasty and carbonated. However, the peak flavor is not reached until one month has elapsed from the time of bottling. This aging, or lagering, is the period during which the hops and malt flavors mellow and the body develops to its full richness and maturity. You may find, as I have, that after three weeks very little of your beer is left to sample, so you may want to brew enough to have a backlog. There have been occasions when I have served my guests beer that has aged only the minimum time, without telling them that I brewed it myself, and in every case they remarked how much richer it tasted than the beer they had been accustomed to. Some people even prefer fresh beer to fully aged beer. Since you are brewing your beer to suit your own taste, the choice is left to you instead of to the breweries.

Many people wonder why home-brewed beer is so much tastier than commercial beer. The following excerpt on brewing and malting from the 1929 edition of the *Encyclopaedia Britannica* should cast some light on the subject:

There are two main methods of bottling beer. In the first, the older and simpler method, the beer is at a certain age after casking merely run into a bottle, stoppered and stored. During storage a slight fermentation takes place in the bottle and these beers have a sediment due to the yeast thus formed. These are called "naturally conditioned beers." In the second method, beer in bulk is surcharged with carbonic acid gas and filtered into bottles, so that there is no sediment. These are the so-called non-deposit beers; this latter class forms the majority of bottled beers.

Naturally Conditioned Beer. Naturally conditioned beers *form the higher classes of pale ales.* The beer is matured in cask before bottling, and this, with subsequent fermentation in bottle, *produces a character which is frequently absent from the non-deposit beers.* The production of these beers requires more technical skill in obtaining just the right quantity of gas in the beer as sold. They require more careful pouring out and there is a certain amount of waste. These points militate against their popularity.*

Since we use the procedure that produces a naturally conditioned beer, we reap the reward of having a richer beer, a beer with much more body and flavor. The slight inconvenience of having to pour slowly and of losing a few drops in the bottom of the bottle is a small price to pay for the enjoyment of such good beer.

The section on procedures would not be complete without a discussion of the differences in preparing home-brewed beer and commercial beer. Commercial breweries treat their beer chemically to keep it from being affected by cold temperatures. This process is called, appropriately enough, chillproofing. It prevents the beer from becoming cloudy when it is cooled to temperatures approaching the freezing point. This procedure is designed to appeal to the eye rather than to the palate, since this clouding over, an enzymatic process, has little effect on the taste. We do not have to bother with chillproofing our beer. For one thing, we don't have to store beer for long periods at very cold temperatures. For another, the process is complicated and expensive. To eliminate the problem of chilling,

* Reprinted from the *Encyclopaedia Britannica* (1929 edition) by permission of the publishers.

don't put the beer into the refrigerator until the day you intend to drink it, ideally around five to six hours before drinking.

It is well known among connoisseurs of fine beverages that as much care must be taken in the serving of beer as in the serving of the finest champagnes. Champagne can be served at a wide range of temperatures. The ideal temperature for beer when served is between 38° and 42°.

The choice of mugs is important also. If you do not have suitable beer mugs, you will want to acquire some. They should be made of heavy glass and have either a handle or a stem, so that the warmth of your hand will not be readily transferred to the beer. Beer mugs should be able to accommodate a twelve-ounce bottle of beer and have enough room left over for a foamy head. Ideally, they should be the same temperature as the beer at the moment of pouring. To accomplish this, put your mugs in the refrigerator about an hour before use. Do not freeze them, as this will ruin any beer. Do not use the mugs for any other beverage and don't use soap to clean them. Rather than drying them with a cloth, allow them to drain dry and store them upside down. If you follow these simple guidelines for the correct serving of beer, the end result will be a more satisfying and enjoyable brew. This applies both to the beer you brew yourself and to the beer you buy from the store.

Because of the small yeast deposit on the bottom of each of your beer bottles, you must pour more carefully than you would a commercial brew, so as not to disturb the deposit and cloud the beer. Pour slowly and try not to bubble the beer at the neck of the bottle. This seems tricky at first, but you will soon get the hang of it. Do not return the bottle to an upright position until you have finished pouring. As you notice the yeast coming forward with the last half ounce or so of beer, stop pouring as it approaches the neck and immediately rinse out the bottle. Since the yeast forms a fairly cohesive layer on the bottom of the bottle, very little of the beer is wasted. If you are pouring from quart bottles, be sure to have three of the mugs lined up side by side so you can pour out the contents continuously without having to raise the bottle and billow the yeast. You may occasionally cloud your beer when pouring, but this is no real problem. The yeast cannot hurt you and is indeed quite nutritious. It will not affect the flavor of the beer in any way. The reason for taking so much care in pouring is purely an aesthetic one. I want my brew to look clear and sparkling.

Now that you have read in detail the procedures for brewing your own beer, you will find the procedure outline accompanying each recipe handy as a reference to use during the actual brewing operation.

Beer Recipes

Basic Recipe

This recipe is the culmination of three years of effort to produce a beer that has a far richer taste than commercial beer, yet retains the refreshing, thirst-quenching quality inherent in the light lagers. This beer has been widely acclaimed as the best ever tasted by those who have sampled it. I strongly recommend that you use this recipe for your initial batch. It will produce a medium-light lager beer with a rich malt taste.

Beadlebrew

INGREDIENTS

5¼ U.S. gallons of water
2 cans Munton & Fison light
    malt syrup
1½ lbs. corn sugar
2 level tsp. salt
1 level tsp. acid blend
2 level tsp. nutrient
1 pack Grey-Owl dried beer
    yeast
½ level tsp. finings
½ level tsp. ascorbic acid
⅖ cup sugar
1 level tsp. spruce essence
    (optional)

EQUIPMENT

Primary fermenter
Secondary fermenter
    (carboy)
2-gallon mixing pot
Extra-wide Saran Wrap or
    plastic sheeting
Masking or Scotch tape
Small saucepan
Siphon hose
Long mixing spoon
Measuring cup
Bottles, caps

1. Fill carboy to 1 inch from top with cold water. Pour 1 gallon of that water into mixing pot and heat to 150°, then remove from heat. Add salt, acid blend, malt. (If dried malt, add first.) Add corn sugar. Stir for 3 minutes.
2. Pour remainder of water from carboy into primary fermenter, add beer mix. Add nutrient, yeast, cover with plastic sheeting, seal with tape.
3. One day after foamy head recedes, siphon into secondary fermenter. Dissolve finings and add during siphoning. Attach fermentation lock. Allow to ferment for 15 days in carboy. Final specific gravity should be 1.008 or lower.
4. Siphon beer into primary fermenter. Add ½ teaspoon of ascorbic acid. Dissolve 2/5 cup of sugar in small saucepan of warm beer, add to rest of beer, mix thoroughly. (If using spruce essence, add 1 teaspoon and mix thoroughly.)
5. Siphon into bottles and cap. Tip each bottle upside down once to wet seal. Store upright at room temperature for at least 15 days.

Beadlebrew Dark

INGREDIENTS

5¼ U.S. gallons of water
2 cans Munton & Fison dark
   malt syrup
1½ lbs. corn sugar
2½ level tsp. salt
1 level tsp. acid blend
2 level tsp. nutrient
1 pack Grey-Owl dried beer
   yeast
½ level tsp. finings
½ level tsp. ascorbic acid
⅖ cup sugar
1 level tsp. spruce essence
   (optional)

EQUIPMENT

Primary fermenter
Secondary fermenter
   (carboy)
2-gallon mixing pot
Extra-wide Saran Wrap or
   plastic sheeting
Masking or Scotch tape
Small saucepan
Siphon hose
Long mixing spoon
Measuring cup
Bottles, caps

1. Fill carboy to 1 inch from top with cold water. Pour 1 gallon of that water into mixing pot and heat to 150°, then remove from heat. Add salt, acid blend, malt. (If dried malt, add first.) Add corn sugar. Stir for 3 minutes.
2. Pour remainder of water from carboy into primary fermenter, add beer mix. Add nutrient, yeast, cover with plastic sheeting, seal with tape.
3. One day after foamy head recedes, siphon into secondary fermenter. Dissolve finings and add during siphoning. Attach fermentation lock. Allow to ferment for 15 days in carboy. Final specific gravity should be 1.008 or lower.
4. Siphon beer into primary fermenter. Add ½ teaspoon of ascorbic acid. Dissolve 2/5 cup of sugar in small saucepan of warm beer, add to rest of beer, mix thoroughly. (If using spruce essence, add 1 teaspoon and mix thoroughly.)
5. Siphon into bottles and cap. Tip each bottle upside down once to wet seal. Store upright at room temperature for at least 15 days.

Ale

Ale has a slightly different taste than beer due to a difference in the type of yeast used in fermentation. Lager beer is made with bottom-fermenting yeast and ale is made with a top-fermenting variety. The procedure is the same, except that the brew made with ale yeast must be skimmed periodically before being added to the secondary fermenter, because top-fermenting yeast forms a pancake of yeast on top of the brew. If this yeast layer is not skimmed, it will eventually settle to the bottom, and this would give the ale a taste that is described by brewmasters as "yeast-bitten." The brew should be allowed to ferment in the primary fermenter two days longer than usual before being transferred to the secondary fermenter, so that most of the yeast can be skimmed. The taste for ale is usually an acquired one, as opposed to the taste for beer, which is more acceptable to the American palate.

Using Your Own Hops

The previous recipes in this book call for the use of a malt extract which is hop-flavored. The use of this malt eliminates the need for us to spend extra time and money adding our own hops to the brew. After trying the standard recipes, some of you may want to add your own hops so that you can get more variation in your recipes or feel that you played a greater part in creating your fine brew. Over the past few years I have experimented with a number of recipes calling for the addition of hops separately, and there is a slight difference in the taste of beer prepared this way as opposed to preparations using hopped malt. It is only fair to say that it is strictly a matter of personal opinion whether the beer is improved by this added step. Some think beer made with hops added separately has more character, and some can detect no difference. The standard method certainly has the advantage of convenience. However, by using your own hops, you can brew a beer as light in color and taste as the commercial variety, since you can use dried light powdered malt exclusively instead of combining it with malt syrup, which has a slightly heavier taste. The hops can be purchased from the wine-makers' supply firms in compressed bricks weighing four ounces and usually costing less than ninety cents.

PROCEDURE

Before adding the beer mix to the rest of the cold water as described in the standard procedure outline, pour about one half gallon of the water into a large saucepan and bring it to a boil. Add one half teaspoonful of salt. Cut off a length of cheesecloth (extra-wide) so that you end up with a large square. Break off one fourth of the hop brick (one ounce) and separate the leaves onto the cheesecloth. In addition, break off and set aside a half ounce of hops to add directly to the water during the last five minutes of boiling. This will add aroma, which is lost from the rest of the hops during the longer boiling period. Tie the hops into a very loose sack (loose, because the hops will expand considerably when boiled), put the sack in the boiling water, and let the hops simmer for twenty-five minutes. This will allow the flavors of the hops to come out into the water in exactly the same manner as a teabag. When the water has cooled sufficiently, wring out the sack into the saucepan to extract any excess water. Put a square of cheesecloth in a mesh strainer and pour the hop liquid through it into the primary fermenter. This will effectively strain out hop residues and fragments of leaves that escaped from the hop sack.

In the following recipes I have indicated that 1½ ounces of hops are to be used. This will give the beer an average bitter taste, so try this amount first. If you find that it is too mild or too bitter for your taste, you can increase or decrease the amount of hops accordingly. Do not vary the amount more than one ounce at a time, as anything under one ounce will produce a very weak and insipid beer and anything over 2½ ounces will produce an exceedingly bitter brew. Hops are very potent and they have a strong odor. If you have an exhaust fan in your kitchen, I recommend that you turn it on when you are working with hops to prevent their pungency from permeating your household.

In recipes that call for six pounds of dried malt you will find that, when dissolving it in the hot water, it will tend to form lumps. Simply stir longer until the lumps are completely blended into the solution.

Light Pilsner

This recipe will produce a pale-light beer similar to that available commercially from the Scandinavian countries.

INGREDIENTS

5¼ U.S. gallons of water
3½ lbs. Munton & Fison
    dried light malt
2½ lbs. corn sugar
1½ oz. hops
2 level tsp. salt
1 level tsp. acid blend
2 level tsp. nutrient
1 pack Grey-Owl dried
    beer yeast
½ level tsp. finings
½ level tsp. ascorbic acid
⅖ cup sugar
1 level tsp. spruce essence
    (optional)

EQUIPMENT

Primary fermenter
Secondary fermenter
    (carboy)
2-gallon mixing pot
Large saucepan
Large sheet of cheesecloth
Extra-wide Saran Wrap or
    plastic sheeting
Masking or Scotch tape
Small saucepan
Siphon hose
Measuring cup
Long mixing spoon
Bottles, caps

1. Fill carboy to 1 inch from top with cold water. Pour 1 gallon of that water into mixing pot and heat to 150°, then remove from heat. Add salt, acid blend, malt. Do not stir until the second bag has been added or the mix will cause the last bagful to lump on the surface. Add corn sugar. Stir for 3 minutes.

2. Pour ½ gallon of water from the carboy into a large saucepan, then pour the remaining water from the carboy into the primary fermenter, add beer mix. Add yeast, nutrient, cover with plastic sheeting. Boil saucepan of water and prepare hops as indicated. Put the saucepanful of hot hop water in the refrigerator until it cools to room temperature, then strain it into the rest of the beer mix as indicated. You must allow the liquid to cool down before adding it or the fermentation will be affected. Cover again with plastic sheeting and seal with tape.

3. One day after foamy head recedes, siphon into secondary fermenter. Dissolve finings and add during siphoning. Attach fermentation lock. Allow to ferment for 15 days in carboy. Final specific gravity should be 1.008 or lower.

4. Siphon beer into primary fermenter. Add ½ teaspoon of ascorbic acid. Dissolve 2/5 cup of sugar in small saucepan of warm beer, add to rest of beer, mix thoroughly. (Optional: add 1 teaspoon of spruce essence and mix thoroughly.)

5. Siphon beer into bottles and cap. Tip each bottle upside down once to wet seal. Store upright at room temperature for at least 15 days.

Munich Dark

INGREDIENTS

5¼ U.S. gallons of water
3½ lbs. Munton & Fison
    dried dark malt
2½ lbs. corn sugar
1½ oz. hops
2 level tsp. salt
1 level tsp. acid blend
2 level tsp. nutrient
1 pack Grey-Owl dried
    beer yeast
½ level tsp. finings
½ level tsp. ascorbic acid
⅖ cup sugar
1 level tsp. spruce essence
    (optional)

EQUIPMENT

Primary fermenter
Secondary fermenter
    (carboy)
2-gallon mixing pot
Large saucepan
Large sheet of cheesecloth
Extra-wide Saran Wrap or
    plastic sheeting
Masking or Scotch tape
Small saucepan
Siphon hose
Measuring cup
Long mixing spoon
Bottles, caps

1. Fill carboy to 1 inch from top with cold water. Pour 1 gallon of that water into mixing pot and heat to 150°, then remove from heat. Add salt, acid blend, malt. Do not stir until the second bag has been added or the mix will cause the last bagful to lump on the surface. Add corn sugar. Stir for 3 minutes.
2. Pour ½ gallon of water from the carboy into a large saucepan, then pour the remaining water from the carboy into the primary fermenter, add beer mix. Add yeast, nutrient, cover with plastic sheeting. Boil saucepan of water and prepare hops as indicated. Put the saucepanful of hot hop water in the refrigerator until it cools to room temperature, then strain it into the rest of the beer mix as indicated. You must allow the liquid to cool down before adding it or the fermentation will be affected. Cover again with plastic sheeting and seal with tape.
3. One day after foamy head recedes, siphon into secondary fermenter. Dissolve finings and add during siphoning. Attach fermentation lock. Allow to ferment for 15 days in carboy. Final specific gravity should be 1.008 or lower.
4. Siphon beer into primary fermenter. Add ½ teaspoon of ascorbic acid. Dissolve 2/5 cup of sugar in small saucepan of warm beer, add to rest of beer, mix thoroughly. (Optional: add 1 teaspoon of spruce essence and mix thoroughly.)
5. Siphon beer into bottles and cap. Tip each bottle upside down once to wet seal. Store upright at room temperature for at least 15 days.

USING HOP EXTRACT

In only a year since the first edition of this book was published, there have been great improvements made in the quality of hop extract now available for the home beer-maker. This is good news for those of you who like to make beer using only dried malt extract, which is unhopped. Instead of having to go through the rather tedious procedure of boiling hops detailed in the previous pages, you simply add the hop extract to your beer mix when you dissolve the malt in the warm water. Hop extract usually comes in two- or four-ounce containers and is simply an emulsion or concentration of pure hop constituents. The strength of the extract varies slightly among the several brands available. For instance, one brand may call for five teaspoons per five-gallon batch, whereas another may specify two ounces for five gallons. This is no problem, however, as each brand specifies on the container the recommended dosage for average tastes. After sampling your first batch, you may want to vary the dosage slightly in succeeding batches to conform to your own tastes. At least one brand of the hop extract requires that it be boiled in a small amount of water prior to adding to the rest of the beer mix in order to release the flavors, but most do not require this step.

Light Lager

INGREDIENTS

5¼ U.S. gallons of water
3 lbs. Munton & Fison dried
 light malt
3 lbs. corn sugar
Hop extract—dosage as
 specified
2 level tsp. salt
1 level tsp. acid blend
2 level tsp. nutrient
1 pack Grey-Owl dried
 beer yeast
½ level tsp. finings
½ level tsp. ascorbic acid
⅖ cup sugar
1 level tsp. spruce essence
 (optional)

EQUIPMENT

Primary fermenter
Secondary fermenter
2-gallon mixing pot
Extra-wide Saran Wrap or
 plastic sheeting
Masking or Scotch tape
Small saucepan
Siphon hose
Measuring cup
Long mixing spoon
Bottles, caps

1. Fill carboy to 1 inch from top with cold water. Pour 1 gallon of that water into mixing pot and heat to 150°, then remove from heat. Add salt, acid blend, malt. Do not stir until the second bag has been added or the mix will cause the last bagful to lump on the surface. Add hop extract as called for on the container. Add corn sugar. Stir for 3 minutes.

2. Pour remainder of water from carboy into primary fermenter, add beer mix. Add yeast, nutrient, cover with plastic sheeting, seal with tape.

3. One day after foamy head recedes, siphon into secondary fermenter. Dissolve finings and add during siphoning. Attach fermentation lock. Allow to ferment for 15 days in carboy. Final specific gravity should be 1.008 or lower.

4. Siphon beer into primary fermenter. Add ½ teaspoon of ascorbic acid. Dissolve 2/5 cup of sugar in small saucepan of warm beer, add to rest of beer, mix thoroughly. (Optional: add 1 teaspoon of spruce essence and mix thoroughly.)

5. Siphon beer into bottles and cap. Tip each bottle upside down once to wet seal. Store upright at room temperature for at least 15 days.

NOTE: Some types of hop extract are added to the mix in step 1 and other types are added in step 4 prior to bottling.

Dark Beer

INGREDIENTS

5¼ U.S. gallons of water
3 lbs. Munton & Fison dried
 dark malt
3 lbs. corn sugar
Hop extract—dosage as
 specified
2¼ level tsp. salt
1 level tsp. acid blend
2 level tsp. nutrient
1 pack Grey-Owl dried
 beer yeast
½ level tsp. finings
½ level tsp. ascorbic acid
⅖ cup sugar
1 level tsp. spruce essence
 (optional)

EQUIPMENT

Primary fermenter
Secondary fermenter
2-gallon mixing pot
Extra-wide Saran Wrap or
 plastic sheeting
Masking or Scotch tape
Small saucepan
Siphon hose
Measuring cup
Long mixing spoon
Bottles, caps

1. Fill carboy to 1 inch from top with cold water. Pour 1 gallon of that water into mixing pot and heat to 150°, then remove from heat. Add salt, acid blend, malt. Do not stir until the second bag has been added or the mix will cause the last bagful to lump on the surface. Add hop extract as called for on the container. Add corn sugar. Stir for 3 minutes.

2. Pour remainder of water from carboy into primary fermenter, add beer mix. Add yeast, nutrient, cover with plastic sheeting, seal with tape.

3. One day after foamy head recedes, siphon into secondary fermenter. Dissolve finings and add during siphoning. Attach fermentation lock. Allow to ferment for 15 days in carboy. Final specific gravity should be 1.008 or lower.

4. Siphon beer into primary fermenter. Add ½ teaspoon of ascorbic acid. Dissolve 2/5 cup of sugar in small saucepan of warm beer, add to rest of beer, mix thoroughly. (Optional: add 1 teaspoon of spruce essence, and mix thoroughly.)

5. Siphon beer into bottles and cap. Tip each bottle upside down once to wet seal. Store upright at room temperature for at least 15 days.

NOTE: Some types of hop extract are added to the mix in step 1 and other types are added in step 4 prior to bottling.

Stout

Stout is the strongest and heaviest of all beers. It originated in the British Isles and is brewed principally in Ireland, where it is considered the national beverage. When a person asks the tavernkeeper in Ireland for "a pint," this can only mean a mug of Guinness stout. The Guinness Brewery was set up in 1759 at St. James's Gate in Dublin by Arthur Guinness. This feisty businessman must have set the record for farsighted optimism when he signed a lease to pay an annual rent of forty-five pounds—for nine thousand years! Within five years after setting up the brewery, stout became the major beer brewed in Ireland and brewing evolved as the leading industry. The production of Guinness stout was threatened in 1773 when the Dublin City Council claimed water rights over the Guinness Brewery and decided to fill in the channel from which the brewery drew its supply. Disputes between corporate and governmental bodies were much more effectively arbitrated in those days. When the sheriff and workmen arrived to carry out the threat, Arthur Guinness grabbed a pickax from one of the workmen, "declaring with much improper language that they should not proceed." The sight of Guinness brandishing a pickax was too much for the sensitive representatives of the City Council, and they hurriedly beat an undignified retreat, never to return. Guinness breweries were set up in several countries over the years and the product gained in popularity, so that today it can be found in most countries in the world. More stores in the United States are stocking stout, attesting to its growing popularity over here.

Stout is a characteristically dark and bitter beer which derives its flavor from the use of dark toasted malt and the more liberal use of hops. When poured, stout forms a thicker and creamier head than beer. Its head also lasts much longer, because more malt is used than in lighter beers and the toasting of the malt, or caramelization, gives rise to more colloid substances, which help retain a good head. The greater concentration of hop resins and oils also contributes to the head retention. For those of you who have a taste for this strong beer, it is possible to make an excellent stout at home. The following recipes give you a complete range of stouts, from very mild to fiercely strong.

Light Mild Stout

INGREDIENTS

5¼ U.S. gallons of water
2 cans Munton & Fison dark
   malt syrup
1½ lbs. Munton & Fison
   dried light malt
Hop extract as specified for
   5 gallons
2½ level tsp. salt
1 level tsp. acid blend
2 level tsp. nutrient
1 pack Grey-Owl dried
   beer yeast
½ level tsp. finings
½ level tsp. ascorbic acid
⅖ cup sugar
1 level tsp. spruce essence

EQUIPMENT

Primary fermenter
Secondary fermenter
2-gallon mixing pot
Extra-wide Saran Wrap or
   plastic sheeting
Masking or Scotch tape
Small saucepan
Siphon hose
Long mixing spoon
Measuring cup
Bottles, caps

1. Fill carboy to 1 inch from top with cold water. Pour 1 gallon of that water into mixing pot and heat to 150°, then remove from heat. Add salt, acid blend, malt. Add dried malt first. Add hop extract as called for on the container. Stir for 3 minutes.
2. Pour remainder of water from carboy into primary fermenter, add beer mix. Add yeast, nutrient, cover with plastic sheeting, seal with tape.
3. One day after foamy head recedes, siphon into secondary fermenter. Dissolve finings and add during siphoning. Attach fermentation lock. Allow to ferment for 15 days in carboy. Final specific gravity should be 1.010 or lower.
4. Siphon beer into primary fermenter. Add ½ teaspoon of ascorbic acid. Dissolve 2/5 cup of sugar in small saucepan of warm beer, add to rest of beer, mix thoroughly. Add 1 teaspoon of spruce essence and mix thoroughly.
5. Siphon beer into bottles and cap. Tip each bottle upside down once to wet seal. Store upright at room temperature for at least 15 days.

Rich Mild Stout

INGREDIENTS	EQUIPMENT

INGREDIENTS

5¼ U.S. gallons of water
2 cans Munton & Fison dark
   malt syrup
1½ lbs. Munton & Fison
   dried dark malt
Hop extract as specified for
   5 gallons
2½ level tsp. salt
1 level tsp. acid blend
2 level tsp. nutrient
1 pack Grey-Owl dried beer
   yeast
½ level tsp. finings
½ level tsp. ascorbic acid
⅖ cup sugar
1 level tsp. spruce essence

EQUIPMENT

Primary fermenter
Secondary fermenter
2-gallon mixing pot
Extra-wide Saran Wrap or
   plastic sheeting
Masking or Scotch tape
Small saucepan
Siphon hose
Long mixing spoon
Measuring cup
Bottles, caps

1. Fill carboy to 1 inch from top with cold water. Pour 1 gallon of that water into mixing pot and heat to 150°, then remove from heat. Add salt, acid blend, malt. Add dried malt first. Add hop extract as called for on the container. Stir for 3 minutes.
2. Pour remainder of water from carboy into primary fermenter, add beer mix. Add yeast, nutrient, cover with plastic sheeting, seal with tape.
3. One day after foamy head recedes, siphon into secondary fermenter. Dissolve finings and add during siphoning. Attach fermentation lock. Allow to ferment for 15 days in carboy. Final specific gravity should be 1.012 or lower.
4. Siphon beer into primary fermenter. Add ½ teaspoon of ascorbic acid. Dissolve 2/5 cup of sugar in small saucepan of warm beer, add to rest of beer, mix thoroughly. Add 1 teaspoon of spruce essence and mix thoroughly.
5. Siphon beer into bottles and cap. Tip each bottle upside down once to wet seal. Store upright at room temperature for at least 15 days.

English Stout

INGREDIENTS

5¼ U.S. gallons of water
3 cans Munton & Fison dark
   malt syrup
2½ level tsp. salt
1 level tsp. acid blend
2 level tsp. nutrient
1 pack Grey-Owl dried beer
   yeast
½ level tsp. finings
½ level tsp. ascorbic acid
⅖ cup sugar
1 level tsp. spruce essence

EQUIPMENT

Primary fermenter
Secondary fermenter
2-gallon mixing pot
Extra-wide Saran Wrap or
   plastic sheeting
Masking or Scotch tape
Small saucepan
Siphon hose
Long mixing spoon
Measuring cup
Bottles, caps

1. Fill carboy to 1 inch from top with cold water. Pour 1 gallon of that water into mixing pot and heat to 150°, then remove from heat. Add salt, acid blend, malt. Stir for 3 minutes.
2. Pour remainder of water from carboy into primary fermenter, add beer mix. Add yeast, nutrient, cover with plastic sheeting, seal with tape.
3. One day after foamy head recedes, siphon into secondary fermenter. Dissolve finings and add during siphoning. Attach fermentation lock. Allow to ferment for 15 days in carboy. Final specific gravity should be 1.012 or lower.
4. Siphon beer into primary fermenter. Add ½ teaspoon of ascorbic acid. Dissolve 2/5 cup of sugar in small saucepan of warm beer, add to rest of beer, mix thoroughly. Add 1 teaspoon of spruce essence and mix thoroughly.
5. Siphon beer into bottles and cap. Tip each bottle upside down once to wet seal. Store upright at room temperature for at least 15 days.

Strong Irish Stout

INGREDIENTS

5¼ U.S. gallons of water
3 cans Munton & Fison dark
  malt syrup
Hop extract as specified for
  5 gallons
2½ level tsp. salt
1 level tsp. acid blend
2 level tsp. nutrient
1 pack Grey-Owl dried beer
  yeast
½ level tsp. finings
½ level tsp. ascorbic acid
⅖ cup sugar
1 level tsp. spruce essence

EQUIPMENT

Primary fermenter
Secondary fermenter
2-gallon mixing pot
Extra-wide Saran Wrap or
  plastic sheeting
Masking or Scotch tape
Small saucepan
Siphon hose
Long mixing spoon
Measuring cup
Bottles, caps

1. Fill carboy to 1 inch from top with cold water. Pour 1 gallon of that water into mixing pot and heat to 150°, then remove from heat. Add salt, acid blend, malt. Stir for 3 minutes.
2. Pour remainder of water from carboy into primary fermenter, add beer mix. Add yeast, nutrient, cover with plastic sheeting, seal with tape.
3. One day after foamy head recedes, siphon into secondary fermenter. Dissolve finings and add during siphoning. Attach fermentation lock. Allow to ferment for 15 days in carboy. Final specific gravity should be 1.012 or lower.
4. Siphon beer into primary fermenter. Add ½ teaspoon of ascorbic acid. Dissolve 2/5 cup of sugar in small saucepan of warm beer, add to rest of beer, mix thoroughly. Add 1 teaspoon of spruce essence and mix thoroughly.
5. Siphon beer into bottles and cap. Tip each bottle upside down once to wet seal. Store upright at room temperature for at least 15 days.

Making a Richer Beer

There is a very subtle taste difference between beer brewed with a combination of dried and canned malt and that produced by the finest European breweries. Our own beer has what can only be described as a lighter taste because we are using pure malt extract, whereas the breweries use mash and steep with whole barley grain. These grains have a small amount of insoluble sugar and starches, and the barley grain husks add a flavor of their own. True connoisseurs of beer can detect and appreciate this subtle difference. Those of you who prefer the thicker and richer imported German beer can achieve this character in your own beer by using the following procedure. This is an advanced beermaking procedure and I recommend that you make a batch or two using the procedures under the standard recipe section before proceeding to this added step. This step is best used in conjunction with the first recipe on page 94 and it will produce a delicious, rich, light lager beer.

First obtain some whole-grain malted barley, which comes in three-pound packages, from a wine-makers' supply firm. Do not confuse this with dried malt extract, as these are the actual hard grains of barley, costing about half what dried malt costs. Measure out one pound per five-gallon batch of beer. This barley is used along with the regular ingredients in the recipe and not in place of them. The grains must first be crushed into small bits, but not powdered, or the beer will not clarify satisfactorily. A food blender on slow speed is excellent for this purpose. Pour one third cup of barley at a time into the blender and turn on for about three seconds. This should be sufficient time to break open all the grains. If more than this amount of barley is added at one time, or if it is crushed for a longer period of time, it will be powdered like flour, which may cause the finished beer to have a slight haze. It is important only that all the grains be broken. A coffee grinder is also satisfactory for crushing the grain. Some people use a rolling pin, but this is a very hard way to do it and not worth the time and trouble.

It is best to prepare this part of your mix several hours before mixing the dried and canned malt. As you will see in the procedure below, the grain must be heated and then allowed to cool before being added to the rest of the recipe. If it is added while hot, two of the 5½ gallons of the mix would be heated instead of just one gallon as under the standard procedure. This would make the entire mix too warm for the yeast, and an interesting but aggravating situation would arise. Initially the yeast would begin fermenting earlier due to the heat, but after it was transferred to the carboy, it would slow down to almost complete inactivity for two weeks and then gradually become more lively and finish working out after a total of four weeks in the carboy. The reason for this phenomenon is that the initial generations of yeast are multiplying in a warm beer mix. After the mix cools down, the yeast has to have time to acclimate itself to a cooler environment. The problem is eliminated before it arises by giving the barley-grain mix time to cool in the refrigerator before adding it to the malt mix.

PROCEDURE

Fill the carboy with water to the standard height along the top seam and pour a gallon out into a large saucepan. Keep the rest of the water in the carboy until later, when you mix the standard part of the recipe. Heat the water in the saucepan to between 151° and 155° F. (using a candy thermometer to measure the temperature). This temperature range is critical for converting the starch in the malted barley into fermentable sugar through the action of the diastase enzyme. Be very careful not to exceed the upper limit of this temperature range. Once the proper temperature has been achieved, a low flame on the center of the burner will be enough to sustain it. Next, pour the crushed barley in a circle around the edge of the pan so that not too much is concentrated in the middle where the heat is higher. To obtain the correct temperature of the barley, leave the thermometer attached to the pan with the end touching the ring of grain. Let the mix simmer at 153° for two hours. During the last two or three minutes, agitate the grains with a spoon or egg-beater to dislodge the malt sugars still adhering to the grains. Bring the solution to a boil, then turn off the stove. When the liquid has cooled to below 90°, pour it into the primary fermenter through a strainer containing a double layer of cheesecloth. Hold back the grains with a spoon if necessary to prevent them from falling out. Add some more water to the grains in the pan, stir, and strain again into the primary fermenter. This is known as "sparging" and it simply rinses more of the malt sugars from the grains to be used in your brew. Proceed with the standard recipe and procedure outline.

The final specific gravity of this beer may be as much as .003 higher than that of the standard recipe. For instance, it may be 1.013 before the priming sugar is added. Since this increase represents some insoluble starches and sugars, it is still safe to bottle after the priming sugar is added. The beer should be aged for three weeks before sampling. After two weeks of storage, you will notice a slight trace of substance floating on top of the beer in each bottle. This is only barley residue and it will sink to the bottom when the neck of each bottle is shaken back and forth a few times.

Again, this procedure is a great deal more time-consuming than the standard recipes. I recommend it only for the serious hobbyist with a taste for European-type beer.

Home-Brew Recipes

The following recipes are similar to those used for years by home-brewers in this country. The main difference between these recipes and all the others in this book is that the home-brew recipes use white household sugar in place of the dried malt extract. The flavor of this beer is not as rich as that of beer made with malt only, and the body is lighter, though many people still prefer it to the commercial variety. Also, the cost is low. Your outlay for all the ingredients and additives for five gallons will be about what you would pay for one six-pack of commercial beer. Who can complain about beer that costs only a few cents a bottle!

Because cane sugar is used in these recipes, the flavor will be slightly cidery. This is due to the fact that, after the yeast has converted the sweetness of the sugar to alcohol and carbon dioxide gas, only the taste of the cane is left, and this affects the overall taste of the brew. For this reason I differentiate between beer, which uses malt and corn constituents as the major ingredient, and home brew, which uses ordinary sugar along with the malt. These home-brew recipes do mellow somewhat if allowed to age for six weeks or longer. The recipes for the medium and dark home brew will produce a heavier and more bitter brew than the light home-brew recipe because of the higher concentration of hops in the Light and Dark malt than in the Pale Dry.

Light Home Brew

INGREDIENTS

5¼ U.S. gallons of water
1 can Blue Ribbon Pale Dry
   malt
3 lbs. (6 cups) sugar
2 level tsp. salt
1 level tsp. acid blend
2 level tsp. nutrient
1 pack Grey-Owl dried beer
   yeast
½ level tsp. finings
½ level tsp. ascorbic acid
⅖ cup sugar
1 level tsp. spruce essence
   (optional)

EQUIPMENT

Primary fermenter
Secondary fermenter (car-
   boy)
2-gallon mixing pot
Extra-wide Saran Wrap or
   plastic sheeting
Masking or Scotch tape
Small saucepan
Siphon hose
Measuring cup
Long mixing spoon
Bottles, caps

1. Fill carboy to 1 inch from top with cold water. Pour 1 gallon of that water into mixing pot and heat to 140°, then remove from heat. Add salt, acid blend, malt, 3 pounds of sugar. Stir for 3 minutes.
2. Pour remainder of water from carboy into primary fermenter, add beer mix. Add yeast, nutrient, cover with plastic sheeting, seal with tape.
3. One day after foamy head recedes, siphon into secondary fermenter. Dissolve finings and add during siphoning. Attach fermentation lock. Allow to ferment for 15 days in carboy. Final specific gravity should be 1.003 or lower.
4. Siphon beer into primary fermenter. Add ½ teaspoon of ascorbic acid. Dissolve 2/5 cup of sugar in small saucepan of warm beer, add to rest of beer, mix thoroughly. (Optional: add 1 teaspoon of spruce essence and mix thoroughly.)
5. Siphon beer into bottles and cap. Tip each bottle upside down once to wet seal. Store upright at room temperature for at least 15 days. It is best to allow home brew to age several weeks, however.

Medium Home Brew

INGREDIENTS

5¼ U.S. gallons of water
1 can Blue Ribbon Extra
    Pale malt
3 lbs. (6 cups) sugar
2 level tsp. salt
1 level tsp. acid blend
2 level tsp. nutrient
1 pack Grey-Owl dried beer
    yeast
½ level tsp. finings
½ level tsp. ascorbic acid
⅖ cup sugar
1 level tsp. spruce essence
    (optional)

EQUIPMENT

Primary fermenter
Secondary fermenter (car-
    boy)
2-gallon mixing pot
Extra-wide Saran Wrap or
    plastic sheeting
Masking or Scotch tape
Small saucepan
Siphon hose
Measuring cup
Long mixing spoon
Bottles, caps

1. Fill carboy to 1 inch from top with cold water. Pour 1 gallon of that water into mixing pot and heat to 140°, then remove from heat. Add salt, acid blend, malt, 3 pounds of sugar. Stir for 3 minutes.
2. Pour remainder of water from carboy into primary fermenter, add beer mix. Add yeast, nutrient, cover with plastic sheeting, seal with tape.
3. One day after foamy head recedes, siphon into secondary fermenter. Dissolve finings and add during siphoning. Attach fermentation lock. Allow to ferment for 15 days in carboy. Final specific gravity should be 1.003 or lower.
4. Siphon into primary fermenter. Add ½ teaspoon of ascorbic acid. Dissolve 2/5 cup of sugar in small saucepan of warm beer, add to rest of beer, mix thoroughly. (Optional: add 1 teaspoon of spruce essence and mix thoroughly.)
5. Siphon into bottles and cap. Tip each bottle upside down once to wet seal. Store upright at room temperature for at least 15 days. It is best to allow home brew to age several weeks, however.

Dark Home Brew

INGREDIENTS

5¼ U.S. gallons of water
1 can Blue Ribbon Dark
  malt
3 lbs. (6 cups) sugar
2 level tsp. salt
1 level tsp. acid blend
2 level tsp. nutrient
1 pack Grey-Owl dried beer
  yeast
½ level tsp. finings
½ level tsp. ascorbic acid
⅖ cup sugar
1 level tsp. spruce essence
  (optional)

EQUIPMENT

Primary fermenter
Secondary fermenter (car-
  boy)
2-gallon mixing pot
Extra-wide Saran Wrap or
  plastic sheeting
Masking or Scotch tape
Small saucepan
Siphon hose
Measuring cup
Long mixing spoon
Bottles, caps

1. Fill carboy to 1 inch from top with cold water. Pour 1 gallon of that water into mixing pot and heat to 140°, then remove from heat. Add salt, acid blend, malt, 3 pounds of sugar. Stir for 3 minutes.
2. Pour remainder of water from carboy into primary fermenter, add beer mix. Add yeast, nutrient, cover with plastic sheeting, seal with tape.
3. One day after foamy head recedes, siphon into secondary fermenter. Dissolve finings and add during siphoning. Attach fermentation lock. Allow to ferment for 15 days in carboy. Final specific gravity should be 1.003 or lower.
4. Siphon into primary fermenter. Add ½ teaspoon of ascorbic acid. Dissolve 2/5 cup of sugar in small saucepan of warm beer, add to rest of beer, mix thoroughly. (Optional: add 1 teaspoon of spruce essence and mix thoroughly.)
5. Siphon into bottles and cap. Tip each bottle upside down once to wet seal. Store upright at room temperature for at least 15 days. It is best to allow home brew to age several weeks, however.

Mead Making

Like beer, mead is a drink whose origins are lost. The ancient Greeks and Romans drank this beverage in great quantities, especially during orgies, since mead was reputed to be a powerful aphrodisiac as well as a delicious, intoxicating brew. It is a drink which has held the highest acclaim of every culture that has produced it. The Greeks considered it the nectar of the gods, and the Anglo-Saxons, not to be outdone, praised it as the drink of kings and thanes. Mead making flourished in England and on the Continent until the late seventeenth century, when sugar from the West Indies came into general use. Honey is a major ingredient in mead, and with the growing popularity of sugar, honey was no longer in demand as a sweetening agent. Production of honey declined and along with it the popularity of mead. This was most unfortunate for those of us who have a taste for this nectar of the gods.

Several different beverages are in the category of true meads. Strictly speaking, mead is made with honey, water, and yeast. This type of mead may take up to a year to ferment and require up to three years to reach its peak flavor. There are other types of mead, just as delicious, which are made with fruits. These are known as melomels, and they require the same amount of time to ferment and age as our wines. The types of melomels which were once made are: pyment, a honey wine produced by a combination of honey and grape juice; hippocras, which is the same as pyment, with spices and herbs added to enhance the flavor; metheglin, made with honey, spices, and herbs; and cyser, made with honey and apples. This last type is the kind we will make, using the following recipe. The alcohol content will be slightly over fifteen percent, and it will be pleasantly sweet. It is excellent as a dessert wine—or as a bedtime cordial, when one can decide for oneself if there is any merit in the qualities attributed to this beverage by the imbibers of ancient Greece and Rome.

The mead base used in the following recipe is a concentrate of apple juice and honey and is available through wine-makers' supply firms.

Mead

INGREDIENTS

38- oz. can mead base
2 level cups sugar
3 level tsp. acid blend
1 level tsp. nutrient
Montrachet wine yeast
⅛ tsp. finings

EQUIPMENT

2 1-gallon glass jugs
1 fermentation lock
Siphon hose
Funnel
5 fifth-size champagne
   bottles with plastic corks

1. Pour can of mead base into thoroughly clean 1-gallon jug. Add 3 teaspoons of acid blend and 1 teaspoon of nutrient. Fill the jug with cold water and shake well to mix the mead base completely into solution. Transfer 1 quart of the mead into a bottle and store it in the refrigerator for use later.

2. Pour ½ pack of Montrachet wine yeast into a cup of water warmed to body temperature (about 100 degrees) and let it sit for 10 minutes to reactivate the yeast. Stir it completely into solution in the cup and add it to the mead in the gallon jug. Shake once to mix and fit fermentation lock to the jug. After 5 days of fermentation, dissolve 2 cups of sugar in warm water. When cool, add to the mead. As the foamy head begins to go down after several more days, add the mead from the quart bottle to top up the jug in stages.

3. After 3 weeks of fermentation, transfer the mead to the other gallon jug, leaving behind the yeast layer on the bottom. Prepare ⅛ teaspoon of finings by dissolving in small amount of warm water. When cool, add to the mead. Top up the jug to within one inch of the lock with cold water. Fit lock to jug. Age until mead is totally clear and all fermentation bubbles have ceased rising to the top. Usually 3 to 6 months. Be sure to check water level in the lock periodically and add more as it evaporates or the mead will spoil from contact with the air. Remove only the cap of the lock to replenish water if needed.

2. When mead has cleared down to the yeast layer, siphon carefully into the other gallon jug, and from there into bottles and seal. Store bottles upright at room tempera-

ture for at least 2 months. Mead improves continuously over a period of a year. The champagne bottles are used in case of slight refermentation as they can withstand great pressure. However, this is highly unlikely to happen. Serve chilled.

Old-Fashioned Cider

It is appalling to me that people will pay $1.25 for a jug of apple cider and then drink it up before it has been blessed by the kiss of the yeast. Apple cider in its un-fermented state ranks with the kiddie drinks and other assorted beverages that fill grocers' shelves. Add a little wine yeast to apple cider and you have an entirely dif-ferent drink. The resulting beverage is delicious, re-freshing, slightly carbonated, and even a little alco-holic. It is now in its natural state, and all the good things of life are better in their natural state.

To make apple cider you will need an ordinary glass gallon jug, a roll of Saran Wrap, a small rubber band, and some dried all-purpose wine yeast. When you buy commercial apple cider, it is not in its natural state, because it is unfermented. Pour out about one quart from a gallon jug to give the foam room to rise. (Later on, you can pour the quart back in to ferment, so save this in the refrigerator.) If your store doesn't carry cider, or stocks it only in the fall, buy four six-ounce cans of frozen apple-juice concentrate and pour the contents into the gallon jug. The instructions on the concentrate will call for adding four cans of water to one of apple juice; ignore this and add only eleven cans of water in order to make the mix a bit richer. Pour in one third of a pack of wine yeast and cover the opening of the jug with a piece of Saran Wrap. Secure it tightly with a rubber band and let the jug sit at room temperature. This covering over the top will act as a low-pressure valve, allowing some of the gas to escape during fermentation but holding in enough to carbonate the cider. Do *not* cap the jug or it will blow up from the pressure.

At normal room temperature the fermentation will start within a day. After one day of active fermentation, place the jug in the refrigerator to cool and slow down the fermentation. When the jug is good and cold you can take off the cover and sample the cider. Cider is the only beverage that tastes good while it is still undergoing active fermentation. It should be served in beer mugs that have been placed in the freezer prior to filling. After pouring, replace the covering over the neck and put the jug back in the refrigerator. The cider will be well carbonated and will have a good head. (It will also be quite cloudy, but this is perfectly normal.) Unless you want a very dry cider, you should drink it all during the first week, for it becomes increasingly less sweet as the yeast works out the sugar.

Cider is a drink for all seasons, but one should make sure that plenty is available as a festive beverage to be served during Thanksgiving and Christmas holidays.

The preceding pages of recipes have included all the major varieties of fermented beverages, from light lager beer to the strongest stout. While the recipes listed are those that have the widest appeal, there are many variations. As you become more experienced as a brewer, you will want to try some variations of your own, such as the use of lesser or greater amounts of malt in your brew, or varying the amount of hop extract to produce a milder- or stronger-tasting beer. One of the great advantages to brewing your own beer is that, with so many recipes to choose from, you will surely come up with a brew that you can call your own. Others who become aware of your brewing skills may decide to try making their own beer. Many communities have started beermaking clubs to further the art. As a brewer of your own fine beers, you will soon find that there is great enthusiasm generated when others become aware of your newly acquired skill.

I hope you will find as much enjoyment in this absorbing hobby as I have.

Equipment Supplies

The following components will enable you to prepare all the recipes listed in this book:

1 *heavy-duty polyethylene primary fermenter*
1 *heavy-duty polyethylene secondary fermenter (5½ U.S. gallons)*
1 *fermentation lock and inert stopper*
1 *precision fermentation hydrometer and jar*
1 *siphon hose*
1 *long-handled bottle brush*

dried fermentation yeast
active dry yeast
nutrient
acid blend
ascorbic acid
fining powder
malt extracts
hop extract
spruce essence
cappers, caps, etc.

For information on obtaining a complete fermentation kit, write to:

Specialty Products International, Ltd.
Box 784
Chapel Hill
North Carolina 27514
Tel.: (919) 929-4277
(Wholesale and retail)